TREVOR HUDSON

Pauses
for Lent

—

40 Words *for* 40 Days

UPPER
ROOM BOOKS®
NASHVILLE

Library of Congress Cataloging-in-Publication Data

Hudson, Trevor, 1951–
  Pauses for Lent : 40 words for 40 days / Trevor Hudson.
    pages cm
  ISBN 978-0-8358-1504-8 (print)—ISBN 978-0-8358-1529-1 (mobi)—ISBN 978-0-8358-1505-5 (epub)
  1. Lent—Meditations. I. Title.
  BV85.H763 2015
  242'.34—dc23

                          2014047973

Contents

INTRODUCTION

"What did you give up for Lent?" I remember the first time as a very young Christ-follower that a fellow Christian asked me that question. He came from a very different church denomination than mine. I must confess I had no idea what he was talking about. I still had so much to learn about the history of my new Christian family. Perhaps, like me, you also don't know much about this season called Lent. Allow me to share with you what I have discovered about Lent, the liturgical calendar, and church history.

The Christian calendar contains different seasons. These seasons are "time-gifts" that the church offers to help us participate more fully in what God has done in human history. For example, most of us are familiar with the gifts of Christmas, Easter, and Pentecost—times when we focus on the birth of Jesus, the resurrection of Jesus, and the giving of the Holy Spirit respectively. Imagine how impoverished our Christ-following would be without these sacred gifts of time during which we give special attention to these unique events.

So what then is Lent all about? Unless we were brought up in the Catholic or the Anglican traditions, our knowledge of this particular season might be limited. Our ignorance has unfortunate consequences—we lose out on a wonderful opportunity to reflect on our lives, to face our addictions to consumer culture, and to become more intentional in our discipleship to Christ. Saddest of all, when we undervalue Lent, we often fail to enter as fully into the transforming possibilities of Jesus' death and resurrection.

Introduction

The first mention of Lent in a church document appears in the Council of Nicaea of 325 CE. This Council produced one of our most important creeds: the Nicene Creed. At that time, Lent referred to a special time of preparation for new converts before they were received into the Christian church on Easter Sunday. Records also indicate that it was a time of preparation for the restoration and reconciliation of those who had denied their faith during the persecution.

Eventually all Christ-followers were encouraged to participate in Lent as a forty-day journey leading up to the events of Good Friday and Easter Sunday. The number forty was not chosen randomly. Forty is a number associated with times of intense spiritual preparation and significant transition in the Bible. Think of the forty years Moses spent in the desert before God called him to the tasks of liberating the Israelites and building a new nation. Think of the forty days Jesus spent in the desert wrestling with temptation before he embarked on his public ministry.

During the forty days of Lent, disciples of Jesus are encouraged to engage in three spiritual practices. These practices are those specifically mentioned by Jesus in the Sermon on the Mount: giving to the poor, prayer, and fasting. (See Matthew 6: 1-18.) In this guide to the Lenten journey, I want to suggest something a little different. My prayer is that this book will maximize the opportunities during the season of Lent for us to deepen our relationships to the Crucified One who lives beyond crucifixion.

How to Use This Book

First, I invite you make a commitment to pause during each day of Lent. You will need to decide what time of day works best for you, how long you can give, and where you will sit for those few minutes. It may be first thing in the morning or when you get to work or just after your children have gone to school or during your lunch break. This art of pausing carves out space in your hectic life for you to listen to God.

Second, I have provided forty words for the forty days of Lent. Each day you will focus on one word, and each meditation comes with a Bible verse and a short reflection. During your daily pause, read the verse aloud a few times, read the brief meditation, and then take some time to think about what God may be saying to you through the word for the day. I am hoping that both the verse and meditation will help you explore the meaning that the word has for you in this season of life. I have also provided longer meditations for each Sunday of Lent, including Easter Sunday, giving you a chance to reflect on the circumstances leading up to Jesus' crucifixion and resurrection.

Third, each word comes with a daily practice. I deliberately suggest practices that will not demand too much extra time. Indeed, more often than not, the practices involve actions you are already doing. I trust that consciously linking these activities to the word for the day will help you to see your daily life as the place where God wants to meet you. After all, Christ calls you to follow him in the mess and muddle of your daily life.

Finally, I hope you will not journey through this book alone. The time-gift of Lent is personal but not private. It is to be received and shared with other friends of Jesus, for when Christ enters your life he always brings his sisters and brothers with him. Lent, therefore, is not only the time when you prepare yourself for a richer, deeper, and more vital encounter with the living Christ but also a time when you open yourself more widely and generously to those companions with whom he wants you to travel along the discipleship road.

In closing, I encourage you to ask two or three others to share in this forty-day Lenten journey. Perhaps once a week you can get together over coffee or before church, reflect together on your experiences of the daily practices, and share how God may be speaking to you through the word for the day. I can assure you that if you were to do this along with others, you will not waste a single day of this life-giving gift of Lent.

DUST

"You are dust, and to dust you shall return."
Genesis 3:19

On the first day of Lent, which the church calls Ash Wednesday, many people have their foreheads crossed with ashes as a reminder that they are creatures of dust. We are fragile, fallible, fallen human beings. From the moment we emerge from our mother's womb, we begin the process of dying.

To think that one day we will be nothing but ashes is a pretty grim reality. Not surprisingly many of us avoid facing this truth. It is not something we want to reflect on or speak about or even read. After all, when we begin to sense how near to nothing we are, we can easily find ourselves in despair. Being born to die is not good news.

However, the fact that we are marked by the sign of the cross tells us we are infinitely more than dust. We are God's beloved, and nothing—not even death—can separate us from God's love through Jesus Christ. Our dust is charged with God's own life-sustaining and death-defeating breath. We are beloved dust.

Daily Practice

Go outside and pick up a handful of soil. As you do this, focus on these two symbols: dust and the cross. Even when you wash off the dust from your forehead, remember the reality of your identity—you are dust redeemed by the cross.

Day 2

RETURN

Return to the LORD, your God,
for he is gracious and merciful.
Joel 2:13

Our lives continually drift away from their true home. We forget we are God's beloved. We forget that we are not God. We succumb to the temptations of money, sex, and power. We ignore the cries of our sisters and brothers. We focus only on ourselves.

During Lent, God calls us home. We remember who we truly are. We let God be God in our lives. We respond to our suffering neighbor. Put simply, we begin again with God.

Only when the fierce love of God, fully revealed in the Crucified One, pierces our hearts do we respond lovingly to God. During Lent, we listen for this good news: God passionately loves us and wants us to come home. Lent invites us to open our lives to this love however far we may have drifted and to return again to the God who longs for us.

Daily Practice

Mediate on the word *return* and ask the Holy Spirit to deepen your awareness of God's love. Be aware of the different ways in which the Divine Love comes to you—the smile of a stranger, the presence of a friend, the beauty of a sunset, the enjoyment of a walk. Before you go to sleep, think back on these gifts of God's love, savor them, and give thanks for them.

CHOOSE

Choose life so that you and your descendants may live,
loving the LORD your God, obeying him, and holding fast to him.
Deuteronomy 30:19-20

Our choices matter because their consequences forever shape our lives as well as the lives of others. When my children were growing up, I would often say to them, "You are free to choose to do anything you want, but you are not free to choose the consequences."

In the midst of the journey through the desert, Moses invites the Israelites to make choices that will lead to life. While they are not in control of what happens to them, they do have control of how they will respond to the events of their lives. The consequences of these choices will ripple throughout their lives and futures.

Lent asks us to examine our choices. In almost every moment of our lives—in our thoughts, our imaginations, our actions, and even our inactions—we make choices that lead either toward life or death. Choosing life involves awareness of those tendencies within us that sabotage our lives and of those that nourish them.

Daily Practice

Make two lists today: "What brings me life?" and "What takes life from me?" Add to the lists throughout the day. At the end of the day, reflect on these two columns and ask God for guidance in choosing life. Give thanks to God for new life that comes through Jesus Christ.

FAST

"But when you fast, put oil on your head and wash your face,
so that your fasting may be seen not by others but by your Father
who is in secret; and your Father who sees in secret will reward you."
Matthew 6:17-18

Throughout the ages, those who have made an impact on their generation for the sake of Christ have fasted. This usually involves going without food for a set length of time. Certainly Jesus assumes that his followers will do this as part of their relationship with God. He says, "When you fast . . . " not "If you fast. . . . "

Fasting is really feasting. It provides us with an opportunity to feast on God's overwhelming goodness and love for us. We do this during our fast by nourishing ourselves on those words that God speaks to us. We learn that we do not live on bread alone but by every word of God.

When Jesus instructs us not to look somber when we fast, he is not inviting us to mislead others. He knows that we won't really be sad. He has learned from his own experience how fasting leads us to those unseen gifts that come only from God.

Daily Practice

Refrain from eating today between mealtimes—or choose a day to fast. Allow your desires for food to deepen your consciousness of the spiritual resources that God gives you to endure other difficult deprivations. Remember this: Fasting means feasting on the words of God.

FIRST SUNDAY OF LENT

Read Mark 1:12-15.

Now after John was arrested, Jesus came to Galilee,
proclaiming the good news of God, and saying,
"The time is fulfilled, and the kingdom of God has
come near; repent, and believe in the good news."
Mark 1:14-15

Another kind of life is available to each one of us, right where we are, right now. This astounding offer lies at the heart of Jesus' message about the availability of the kingdom of God. Jesus brings us not so much a new piece of advice or a new social agenda or a new kind of spirituality but a new kind of life.

How can we describe life in the kingdom? It is an intimate life in which we come to know God personally as Abba. It is a shared life through which we come to discover ourselves as a part of God's family. It is a transformational life in which we are gradually changed into the people that God wants us to be. It is a powerful life in which God acts together with us for the good of others and the healing of our world. It is a loving life in which we become more responsive to those around us. Above all, it is an eternal life that cannot be snuffed out by death.

We deeply long for life in the kingdom. This longing is written in capital letters in the hollows of our souls, in the pain of our relationships, and in the strife in our communities. In spite of the abundance of techniques for self-fulfillment and self-help, we still witness and experience despair, addiction, and what seems a tragic inability to get along with those closest to us. We do not appear to live well.

To enter the joy of life in the kingdom, we need to open ourselves to repentance and trust. We must walk a daily journey of turning toward the risen Christ and learning from him how to live our lives. As we do this, he steps out from the pages of the Gospels as our ever present companion and gives us the courage to follow him.

STILL

"Be still, and know that I am God!"
Psalm 46:10

We often place magnets proclaiming this verse in Psalms on our fridges. But there is a huge difference between sticking this verse on the fridge and living it out. Finding stillness and silence in a world conditioned to noise, busyness, and words is not easy. Little wonder we often lack personal and intimate knowledge of the Eternal One.

The psalmist emphasizes that we need to be still to know God. Perhaps this is why our souls yearn for stillness. In their restlessness they long for that silent communion with God for which they are created. Aware of this, Desmond Tutu writes, "Each one of us wants and needs to give ourselves space for quiet." It is in stillness we come to know what our hearts long for: the Divine Presence alive in us. In this way, we can see the importance of fostering a life of outer and inner stillness.

Daily Practice

We can experiment with stillness and silence by purposefully not listening to our car radios or music as we drive or ride the bus or subway. These modes of transport will become mobile places of stillness where we can enter the quietness with God in the midst of the daily rush. Remind yourself that God meets you in the silence.

L O V E

Let us love, not in word or speech,
but in truth and action.
1 John 3:18

We often think of love as a certain kind of feeling. But if we wait for loving feelings, we may never get around to actually loving. On the other hand, when we perform a loving deed, the loving feelings often come along as well.

These loving deeds need not be big. We choose to act in love by taking small steps whenever we can. A smile, a handshake, a hug, a phone call, a greeting, a visit—these are little steps toward love. "Each step," writes Henri J. M. Nouwen, "is like a candle burning in the night."

Lent invites us to practice loving. God passionately loves us—not for us to save it all up in our hearts but to give it away to those around us. We can begin right now, right where we are, with the people nearest us.

Daily Practice

Ask for God's direction in taking small steps of love today. Begin with your closest neighbors or those with whom you live and then include each person who crosses your path today. Consciously fill the day with the light of loving deeds, however small, wherever you go.

LIGHT

Again Jesus spoke to them, saying, "I am the light of the world.
Whoever follows me will never walk in darkness
but will have the light of life."
John 8:12

Darkness resides around and within us. We experience different kinds of darkness: the darkness of intense pain and suffering, the darkness of loneliness and grief, the darkness of evil and sin, and most especially the darkness of death itself. Being overwhelmed by darkness can cause difficulty, confusion, and pain.

Christ enters the darkness of our world as the light. His life both echoes and fulfills the prophecy of Isaiah: "The people who walked in darkness have seen a great light" (9:2). Right up to the present moment, the radiant light of Christ continues to shine among us.

When we follow Christ, his light penetrates our darkness. It illuminates our lives with his direction, delivers us from dark powers, and empowers us to live fuller and freer lives. Indeed, we become children of light in a darkened world!

Daily Practice

Light a candle in a working space or somewhere in your home as a reminder of the good news of John 8:12. Ask yourself, *What are the dark areas in my life?* Bring these areas to the living Christ and let the light of Christ that the darkness has never extinguished shine in.

SEE

"Though I was blind, now I see."
John 9:25

We desire to see and to be seen. How often have we said to absent loved ones, "It would be so good to see you again"? We also want others to seek our presence. Feeling unnoticed or ignored can be very painful. An elderly person expressed her pain to me: "People walk past me as though I am invisible."

Christian faith involves a new way of seeing. When Jesus becomes part of our lives, we see people and things more clearly in our world. John Newton, the converted slave owner and hymn writer, described his inner transformation in these words: "Was blind, but now I see."

God's grace opens blind eyes so that they might see with the eyes of Christ. So let's reflect on our spiritual eyesight. Do our hurried lives make everything and everyone a passing blur? Is it time for our eyes to be touched by Christ? May our eyes become more and more like his, eyes that can truly see others for who they are.

Daily Practice

Look out your window today at God's creation. Let you eyes focus on something of beauty. Look at the people you meet today and see in their faces the beauty of their God-given uniqueness. Give thanks throughout the day for the gift of new eyes that Christ gives to us.

A S K

"Ask, and it will be given you."
Matthew 7:7

"Ask," Jesus teaches, "and it will be given you." This teaching applies both to the way we approach others and the way we approach God. As Dallas Willard points out, "How beautiful it is to see relationships in which asking and receiving are a joyful and loving way of life."

Asking for what we need does not mean we get everything we ask for. But through asking, we learn humility, discover our interdependence, and allow both others and God to show their care for us. It is the way our relationships with God and one another become more real, honest, and intimate.

Asking may prove difficult for some of us. As we grow up, we tend to hide our real needs. Because we want to look strong, in control, and self-sufficient, we don't ask. Lent challenges us to become aware of our need for God's grace and help. It invites us to truly see how needy we are, to stop pretending, and to ask.

Daily Practice

Ask for help either from God or from a trusted friend in something today about which you are struggling and anxious.

WORDS

*"I tell you, on the day of judgment you will have
to give an account for every careless word you utter."*
Matthew 12:36

Words carry much spiritual power. They wound and heal. They
break down and build up. They discourage and encourage. Jesus
places eternal value on them when he says we will be judged by
the words we have spoken. Words are always more than words.

We dare not underestimate the damage that harmful words
cause. They can destroy confidence, tarnish reputations, spread
rumors, split families, divide communities, and spark wars. The
old saying "Sticks and stones can break my bones, but words
will never hurt me" is a lie.

In contrast, helpful words of love and appreciation have the
potential to bring blessing and life. They can make God's love
real for those around us. During Lent, let us think carefully
about how we speak to others.

Daily Practice
Make today a Lenten blessing day. Consciously use words in
ways that heal, build up, and encourage. Seek to do this in as
many conversations as you can during the day.

SECOND SUNDAY OF LENT

Read Mark 3:19-27.

And [Jesus] called them to him, and spoke to them in parables,
"How can Satan cast out Satan? If a kingdom is
divided against itself, that kingdom cannot stand."
Mark 3:23-24

Overcoming evil is an essential ingredient in the life of Jesus. Not only does he conquer evil in the midst of personal temptation, but he also constantly wrenches men and women free from malignant evil whenever it manifests itself in human suffering and pain. Jesus, according to the New Testament writers, is the Divine Agent sent into this world to liberate human beings from the bonds of evil in its many different forms.

Not surprisingly, as we see in our reading, his opponents don't like this. They accuse him of being in league with the demon Beelzebul. Even at this very early stage in Jesus' ministry, naysayers are already looking for a reason to do away with him. Gospel-writer Mark wants to show that the shadow of the cross is beginning to fall across Jesus' life long before the events of Golgotha.

But Jesus responds differently to his opponents' tactics. He refuses to respond to evil with the weapons of evil. He simply points out that their accusations are not logical. If Satan is driving out Satan, then the Evil One is fighting against itself.

Instead, Jesus overcomes evil and brings God's kingdom of freedom to all who are held captive by its dark powers.

How do we share in this victory today? We can face the darkness within our lives honestly and name it for what it is. We can confess our complicity in the societal evils around us. We can call out for the crucified and risen One to deliver us. We can take action against the injustice around us. Most of all, we can keep on demonstrating the power that is stronger than evil: the power of self-giving and crucified love.

ABBA

"Abba, Father, for you all things are possible."
Mark 14:36

Abba is the special word Jesus uses to address God. Roman Catholic priest Albert Nolan points out, "As a way of addressing and referring to God, it was unique." This term combines deep reverence, warm intimacy, and confident trust that displays the kind of relationship Jesus shares with his heavenly Parent.

But Jesus takes this term one step further. Not only does Jesus express this familial relationship with God, but he also wants his followers to do the same. When they pray, Jesus tells his disciples to say, "Father." They can share in the same kind of intimate relationship with God that Jesus has.

The wonderful news is that we can too! When we open our hearts to the Spirit of Jesus, we are enabled to cry out, "Abba." Now we also can begin to live as Abba's children, knowing we are deeply loved and cherished, held in that timeless embrace from which we can never be separated.

Daily Practice
Take this word *Abba* into all your activities today. Whisper it often to express your heart's intention to be in touch with God in the middle of all you do.

Day 12

BREAD

"Give us this day our daily bread."
Matthew 6:11

In the prayer that Jesus teaches his disciples, he invites them to ask for daily bread. This request points us toward our utter dependence on God for sustaining our lives. This phrase emphasizes God's provision—God offers us what we really need on a daily basis.

What are those specific things that we honestly need right now? To ask for these things is what beloved children do naturally when they turn to the one they call Father. We simply ask our heavenly Parent for what we need for today or we ask for what we need now.

Of course, when we pray like this, we must also look beyond ourselves and our own needs. It is impossible to pray for our daily bread without the painful awareness of those who don't have any bread at all. The act of praying for our daily bread encourages us to acknowledge our hungry neighbor.

Daily Practice

At one mealtime today, cut a slice of bread. As you eat it, give thanks to God who sustains you with every breath you take.

WATER

*"Everyone who drinks of this water will be thirsty again,
but those who drink of the water that I will give them
will never be thirsty. The water that I will give will become
in them a spring of water gushing up to eternal life."*
John 4:13-14

Water is one of the most powerful images that Jesus uses to describe himself. When Jesus calls himself our "living water," he means he satisfies our deepest thirsts. Not only does this water quench our thirst but it also becomes like a spring bubbling up inside of us, filling us with the life God wants to give us.

For what do we thirst? Theologian and humanitarian Jean Vanier points out that to be thirsty in biblical language is to be "dried up inside," "to feel totally empty and in anguish." To be thirsty is to long for love, acceptance, and affirmation. In other words, it is to thirst for a heart-to-heart connection with the living and loving God.

Jesus invites those who thirst to come to him and drink his life-giving water. To drink from Jesus is to receive his Spirit in our lives. The water Jesus offers makes our lives new.

Daily Practice
Whenever you drink water today, say this prayer: "Lord, in my thirst for you, give me your water of life." Every sip of water can serve as a reminder of the living water of Jesus.

TIME

*"The time is fulfilled, and the
kingdom of God has come near."*
Mark 1:15

The Greek New Testament uses two words for time: *chronos* and *kairos*. The first word refers to clock time, chronological time. This is time measured in seconds, minutes, hours, days, weeks, months, and years. We refer to *chronos* when we ask someone, "What time is it?"

The second word, *kairos*, refers to God's time, time in the sense of divine destiny. Jesus often speaks of time in this way—"The time is fulfilled," "My hour has not yet come," or "The time is coming when. . . ." He sees his whole life as fulfilling God's destiny, completing the work he was sent to do.

Too often we live our lives determined only by *chronos* time. We forget about the importance of *kairos* time. But what would it mean for us to give attention to both kinds of time? Perhaps our short time here on earth would become charged with eternal significance!

Daily Practice

Finish this sentence each time you check the time today: "In my life right now, it is God's time for. . . ."

PEACEMAKER

"Blessed are the peacemakers."
Matthew 5:9

Despite constant talk of the value of peace, we find very little in this world. Both our public and personal lives reflect our tragic lack of peace—spiraling cycles of violence, unhealthy addictions, and destructive tensions that divide families, communities, and countries. We are far better at loving the idea of peace than at making peace within the realities of our lives.

So our need for peace cries out to heaven as one of the deepest yearnings of the human heart. We seek different kinds of peace—the peace of no longer being suffocated by addiction and anxiety, the peace of being removed from violence and division, the peace of freedom from fear and injustice. We long for God's shalom that the ancient prophets proclaim.

Lent is a good time to pray the prayer of Saint Francis: "Lord, make me an instrument of Thy peace. Where there is hatred, let me sow love. Where there is injury, pardon." Peace spreads when we turn this prayer into deliberate action. Then we make the transition from peace-lovers to peacemakers.

Daily Practice

Think of someone with whom you are not on good terms. Ask God, "Lord, how can I be a peacemaker in this relationship?" Seek God's guidance in the role of peacemaker.

WORLD

*"For God so loved the world that
he gave his only Son."*
John 3:16

Sometimes we make the gospel too small. We reduce it to individuals being reconciled to God or even to God forming a special community. But God's work goes far beyond those acts. God's plan includes the healing of the whole world.

God's loving arms surround the globe. They embrace every human being, nation, and culture. They embrace the trees, mountains, rivers, and every living thing. God wants to rescue, restore, and reconcile the whole world.

God invites us to be part of this divine dream. We cannot take on all human needs and struggles, but we can serve God by taking a small role in healing and reconciliation wherever our lives take us.

Daily Practice

Today when you read the newspaper, read it through the eyes of Jesus. When you watch the nightly news, ask Jesus what breaks his heart. What is God laying on your heart about the world? How are you called to respond?

THIRD SUNDAY
OF LENT

Read Mark 8:27-33.

"But who do you say that I am?"
Mark 8:29

Midway through Mark's Gospel, the mood suddenly changes. During the first eight chapters, we can feel the energy, excitement, and action. Jesus moves from village to village proclaiming the availability of another kind of life, liberating those enslaved by evil, healing the sick, feeding the hungry, and stilling storms and seas. Jesus bears the fruit of a successful ministry. Then comes an abrupt shift in atmosphere. As Eugene Peterson observes, the last eight chapters are dominated by death talk rather than talk about life.

This turning point revolves around a direct question put by Jesus to his disciples, "Who do you say that I am?" Few questions are more important. Is Jesus a myth created by the imaginings of the Gospel writers—some sort of superhero figure able to swoop down into our lives and sort everything out? Is Jesus a great human teacher able to perform miracles? Our response will shape our lives more than our answers to any other question with which we are faced.

When Jesus initially asks this question, Peter blurts out, "You are the Messiah." This response, at this stage of Mark's Gospel, is not a declaration that Jesus is divine or the second part of the Trinity or God. This fuller understanding of Jesus will come later. Here Peter is declaring that Jesus is indeed the One for whom his people have waited so long, the true Servant-King who will usher in God's reign both for Israel and the world. What Peter does not know is that his declaration will turn his life upside down from that time on.

Now it is our moment to wrestle with this question. Who do we say Jesus is? Are we willing, with Peter, to affirm that he is the One for whom our hearts also yearn? Will we also acknowledge him to be the One who alone can heal and empower the human condition? And will we dare to allow him to change our understanding of what it means to follow him today? We can be very sure that if we do call him the Christ and embrace his way of death and resurrection for our lives, it will turn our lives upside down too.

TREASURE

"For where your treasure is,
there your heart will be also."
Matthew 6:21

Each one of us has treasures. As young children, our treasures might have been a special toy, stuffed animal, or blanket. As adults, we continue to have treasures. But now they might be a bank account, a car, or a house.

Jesus teaches that we can store treasures either on earth or in heaven. Earth's treasures pass away. On earth, "moth and rust consume" and "thieves break in and steal" (Matt. 6:19). Or we could say earth is where stock markets crash, computer files corrupt, and accidents damage.

Heaven's treasures, on the other hand, are eternal. We invest in heavenly treasures when we invest in God's work in the lives of others and in the care of all created things.

Daily Practice

As a sign of your intention to invest in treasures of heaven, make today a no-shopping day. Instead, spend the time that you would have spent in shops doing something special for someone else. Be thoughtful and intentional about serving others.

Day 18

LISTEN

Let everyone be quick to listen, slow to speak.
James 1:19

The German theologian and martyr Dietrich Bonhoeffer once wrote, "Many people are looking for an ear that will listen. They do not find it among Christians, because these Christians are talking when they should be listening."

Listening lies at the heart of life with God. But in order to listen to God, we need to learn how to listen to the person next to us. After all, how can we listen to God, whom we cannot see, if we cannot listen to the person we can see?

Lent can be a time when we embark on a spiritual adventure in learning to listen. We can begin this exercise with those closest to us—our colleagues at work, family members, or friends. Listening will become a spiritual practice, an everyday habit, a way of life.

Daily Practice
Ask God today for the gift of ears. Throughout the day remember James's invitation to be quick to listen and slow to speak. Make a conscious effort in every conversation to listen more than you usually do.

Day 19

POOR

"He has anointed me to bring good news to the poor."
Luke 4:18

The word *poor* appears many times in the Bible. Throughout the Old Testament, the poor have a special place in God's heart. In the Psalms, God rescues the poor, defends the poor, and hears their cry. Not surprisingly, Jesus places sharing the good news with the poor at the top of his priorities for ministry.

The devastating suffering of poverty causes God to weep. Sharing God's grief means we act in whatever ways we can to bridge the gap between the rich and poor. In this way, we can embody Jesus' good news for the poor.

Lent challenges us to examine how we relate to those who are impoverished. We can ask ourselves, *Who do I know personally who suffers from poverty?*, *What can I learn from the poor?*, and *How is God calling me to help in efforts aimed at alleviating poverty?* Questions like these lead us into a greater faithfulness to God whose heart is always turned toward the poor.

Daily Practice

As a practical expression of your desire to share God's heart for the poor, make a small donation today to a nongovernmental organization (NGO) that works alongside the economically poor.

FORGIVEN

"Friend, your sins are forgiven."
Luke 5:20

Our most grievous sins occur when we fail to love. We let people down; we hurt others; we offend; we are unresponsive to the needs of others. In all these failures—and in countless others—we behave in unloving ways that break God's heart. When we have sinned, we can ask God for forgiveness.

The good news is that God is more eager to forgive us than we will ever know. God is always there to embrace us, to receive us home again, and to let us start afresh. We see this clearly in the ways Jesus constantly offers forgiveness to those around him who have failed.

One reason we struggle to forgive others is that we do not really believe that we are forgiven people. If we could fully accept the truth that we are forgiven and we don't have to live in shame and guilt, we would know the freedom to forgive. As a forgiven people, we possess the power of forgiveness.

Daily Practice

Take time today to kneel in God's presence. Share your failures as honestly as you can with God. Hear the words of Jesus: "Friend, your sins are forgiven." Receive this forgiveness and step into the new life God offers. If you need to make amends with someone, commit yourself to doing so as soon as possible.

PEACE

"Peace I leave with you; my peace I give to you."
John 14:27

We experience two different kinds of peace. One kind is the peace the world gives. This refers to those fleeting feelings of contentment when everything in life is going well. We feel a pleasurable sense of well-being. There is nothing wrong with this type of peace, but we all know that it can pass very quickly.

The other kind of peace is the one God offers to us. It is a lasting peace that cannot be taken be away from us. It does not depend on our lives running smoothly. God's peace provides an inner assurance that, ultimately, all will be well. This peace occurs in the presence—not the absence—of upheaval and turmoil.

We observe the most obvious example of God's peace in the life of Jesus. For most of Jesus' life, the odds are stacked against him. Tested, tried, and taunted, Jesus maintains an inner serenity through it all. He knows instinctively that because he trusts God completely, all will be well—even when things aren't in the moment. This is the peace that God offers to us.

Daily Practice

Find a quiet place today and hear Christ speak these words into your life in spite of your circumstances: "Peace I leave with you; my peace I give to you." Receive this peace so that you can embody it for those around you.

REST

*"Come to me, all you who are weary
and burdened, and I will give you rest."*
Matthew 11:28, NIV

Most of us know what it means to feel fatigued. Fatigue ambushes us when we work too hard, when we get up too early and go to bed too late, when we try balance too many demands, or when relationships cause conflict and pain. It comes when we live beyond our physical, emotional, and spiritual means.

In the midst of our daily slog, Jesus wants to gift us with rest. Jesus knows the importance God places on rest. After all, not only did God model rest in the creation story but God also demands we rest too.

Rest has many different ingredients. Besides stopping work and learning to relax, it also includes getting adequate sleep. When we do this, we find that we live more joyful, creative, and fruitful lives. When we don't, fatigue takes over and brings failure in many areas of our tired lives.

Daily Practice

Memorize today's verse and repeat it often as you go about your daily work. Go to sleep at a reasonable time tonight and receive your night's rest as a gift from God.

FOURTH SUNDAY OF LENT

Read Mark 9:2-10.

Six days later, Jesus took with him Peter and James and John, and led them up a high mountain apart, by themselves. And he was transfigured before them, and his clothes became dazzling white.
Mark 9:2-3

The details of the Transfiguration are both straightforward and staggering. Jesus and three disciples go up a mountain to pray. As Jesus prays, his appearance changes. He becomes visibly radiant as if the light of heaven shone out of him. Then two ancient biblical figures, Moses and Elijah, appear and talk with him. Finally a cloud covers them, and the disciples became frightened. A voice comes out of the cloud and says, "This is my Son, the Beloved; listen to him!" (v. 7). Then suddenly, the disciples find themselves alone with Jesus again.

This experience stresses two essential truths for our journey in the kingdom of God. First, as Christ-followers we need mountaintop experiences to keep our discipleship fresh, vital, and alive. The eternal realm, the hidden dimension of God's transforming presence, penetrates our earthly reality and is always available to us. We need to regularly open ourselves to this divine reality so that our lives also glow with God's presence and power. If we have never experienced an encounter like this, we may want to reexamine those spiritual practices of solitude, prayer, and worship that open our lives to them.

Second, the Transfiguration reminds us that mountaintop experiences are not ends in and of themselves. Their importance lies in where they lead us. Immediately after Jesus is transfigured, he comes down from the mountaintop into the valley of human need and suffering. He brings healing to a child suffering from seizures. In that moment he translates his spiritual experience into compassionate action. For Jesus, coming down from the mountain is as important as going up the mountain.

Let us take time to ponder this truth. As followers of Jesus, we are invited to bring the light of our mountaintop experiences into the darkness of our pain-filled world. Sometimes we don't want to look at the pain and misery around us—at home, at work, among our neighbors and friends. After all, we live in a culture that works to avoid or ignore others' suffering. But we need to be sharply countercultural. Rather than avoiding them, we need to intentionally engage those who suffer. We can make new beginnings this Lent by connecting with those who are hurting and by offering them the healing beam of God's presence.

WEPT

Jesus wept.
John 11:35, NIV

Each one of us sits next to a pool of our own tears. Our pools are all different. Some have been caused by what has been done to us; some are the results of our own doing. These pools remind us of the grief and losses we have suffered throughout our lives.

Jesus grants us the gift of his own tears. His tears remind us that God weeps with us, grieves with us, and suffers with us. Those who travel the Lenten journey in Jesus' intimate company discover that his tears represent the empathy of God.

Let's consider our own pools of tears. These pools could be caused by the death of a loved one, the pain of a divorce, the abuse of a child, the unmet longing for an intimate partner, the loss of a job, or the rejection from a close friend. Whatever it may be, this pool of tears is where Christ wants to meet us during the season of Lent.

Daily Practice

Take some time today to be alone with the Lord. Share aloud your pool of tears and listen to what God has to say in response.

BUT

*"Everyone who believes in him may not perish
but may have eternal life."*
John 3:16

The verse from the Gospel of John reminds us that a word does not need to be long in order to be important. *But* is a very short word, yet it is essential in grasping the hopeful message of Good Friday and Easter Sunday. In fact, it almost sums up what these two days are all about.

God knows there is a Good Friday side to life. We sin, we hurt one another, and we die—all parts of the failing and futile reality in which we live. If they were the only parts and if sin and death had the final word, life would be terribly despairing and dismal.

But we also experience an Easter side to human life. God does not abandon us to the grave. God's care for us is so great that God comes to us in Jesus Christ so that those who believe in him will not perish but share in the undying life that God gives.

Daily Practice

Every time you use the word *but* today in a sentence, remind yourself of God's gift of love and eternal life.

WAY

"I am the way."
John 14:6

Lent provides us with an opportunity to find our way again. Every day we use pathways, walkways, motorways, driveways, and highways whenever we want to go somewhere. Even with these trails as our guides, we can get lost.

Two thousand years ago when Jesus came into our world, he offered himself to lost humanity as "the way." Just a few years later, the earliest followers of Jesus began calling themselves "people of the Way." (See Acts 9:2.) When we follow Jesus, we enter into a lifelong journey in his company.

Lent encourages those of us who feel lost to get our lives back on track. It turns us toward Christ who meets us where we are, offers his life as the way, and invites us to follow.

Daily Practice
Wherever you walk, run, cycle, or drive today, affirm who you are as a follower of Christ: You are a person of the Way. What does it mean for you to walk in Jesus' company?

FREE

*"If you continue in my word, you are
truly my disciples; and you will know the truth,
and the truth will make you free."*
John 8:31-32

One of the great hymns that Charles Wesley wrote during the eighteenth-century Evangelical Awakening in England contains this line: "My chains fell off, my heart was free, I rose, went forth, and followed Thee." These words give us a glimpse of the radical freedom Jesus promises to his followers.

Christ frees us from those chains holding our lives in bondage—the chains of fear, addiction, and evil—from which we seek release. Christ also frees us for a new life of discipleship, obedience, and adventure. We are set free to love, to praise, and to serve God with our whole being.

When we follow Christ, he liberates us from our shackles to become the people that God wants us to be. This is the glorious freedom offered to the children of God!

Daily Practice
Consider this question today: What addictions and unhealthy attachments keep me from experiencing freedom in Christ?

SIN

*If we say that we have no sin, we deceive
ourselves, and the truth is not in us.*
1 John 1:8

Sin is a three-letter word that we do not like to use today.
Many years ago a psychiatrist named Karl Menninger wrote a
book titled *Whatever Became of Sin?* The book underlined the
importance of rediscovering sin as a concept that helps explain
the mess we have made of our world and of so many of our
relationships.

Sin, biblically understood, is rebellion against God. Usually
this rebellion takes the shape of our refusal to love. We prefer
to go the way of selfishness and self-centeredness. The results of
this tragic rebellion lie all around us in our broken relationships,
broken communities, and broken nations.

Lent provides a wonderful opportunity to let the unself-
ish and other-centered kind of love that took Jesus to the cross
flow more freely throughout our lives. Then our broken lives will
overflow in love toward God and our neighbor.

Daily Practice
One practical way for the love of Christ to flow through you is
to extend forgiveness to someone who has hurt you. Think of
a person today to whom you might offer forgiveness. How can
you show the love of Christ to this person?

Day 28

ENEMIES

*"But I say to you, Love your enemies and pray
for those who persecute you, so that you may be
children of your Father in heaven."*
Matthew 5:44-45

We all have enemies. Sometimes we don't like to admit this. We want to think that we love everyone and that everyone loves us, but that is highly unlikely. Sometimes these enemies pop up even in our family circle!

One of the most difficult challenges for a Christ-follower is loving his or her enemies. Not only does Jesus do this but he also wants us to do so. Obviously Jesus believes that there can be little spiritual growth until we start to love those whom we consider enemies.

Often the first step in loving enemies is praying for them. Praying for our enemies discourages us from saying or doing anything nasty to those we dislike. Prayer also has the power to change our attitudes. Maybe this is why Jesus specifically tells his disciples to pray for their enemies.

Daily Practice

Pick someone today with whom you are not on speaking terms. Take a few minutes to pray specifically for God's blessing on his or her life.

FIFTH SUNDAY OF LENT

Read Mark 10:32-45.

"But whoever wishes to become great among you must be your servant, and whoever wishes to be first among you must be slave of all."
Mark 10:43-44

When Jesus teaches his disciples about what it means to follow him, he redefines the meaning of true greatness. We see this in our reading for today. When James and John ask him if they both can sit alongside him when he comes into glory, he turns their ideas about human greatness upside down. He tells them that they do not know what they are requesting. Jesus explains that those who are considered great by the world's standards hold their power over others. For his followers, however, things are to be totally different. Those who are truly great in the kingdom of God serve others.

The disciples have a difficult time grasping Jesus' view of greatness; so do we. Our society bombards us with completely opposite messages. Those considered great are people with power, people continually in the public spotlight, and people served by others. But the way of Jesus, as we have seen, is radically different. Jesus encourages us to serve others without taking credit and to choose last place over the front of the line. It sounds crazy, and so we mutter under our breath, "Why on earth should we even consider doing this?"

The reason is clear. We travel this path because it is Jesus' way into the kingdom. If we want to experience the life that God makes possible, we must take this path of servanthood. We have to learn how to give up the right to be in charge, to call the shots, to give the orders. Rather, we seek to discover how to become available to others, to bless those near us, to be sensitive to the needs in our midst. In the process, we come to experience the gift of another kind of life, a life of joyful freedom and gradual transformation, a life in the kingdom of God.

Each of us needs to explore what Jesus' instructions mean for us. Most certainly it will mean joining those who our society does not consider important—the destitute, the desperate, the elderly, the homebound, the sick, the victims—and learning how best to serve them.

SERVE

*"The Son of Man came not
to be served but to serve."*
Matthew 20:28

Jesus calls his followers to be servants. When we open our lives to him, his Spirit will always lead us into the position and posture of service. Serving others is the badge of genuine discipleship.

Jesus himself models service when he washes the dirty feet of his disciples. Through this act, Jesus gives the disciples a pattern to follow. He says to them, "I have set you an example, that you also should do as I have done to you" (John 13:15). We find nothing optional about Jesus' words. They are clear, direct, and invite our response.

Serving others the way Jesus would have us do can take many differing forms: offering a ride, taking time to listen to a friend or coworker, babysitting for a single parent, taking out the trash, washing the dishes, and so on. These acts may seem small, but believe me, they can make a big impression on the people we serve!

Daily Practice

Experiment throughout the day with this prayer: *Lord, please bring someone across my path today whom I can serve.*

MONEY

"You cannot serve both God and money."
Matthew 6:24, NIV

Money is a touchy subject. Even though it plays a massive part in our personal and social lives, we find it difficult to talk openly about how our faith relates to our money. Indeed, many of us find ourselves stuck in secret and hidden financial obsessions.

In contrast to our reticence and reserve, Jesus talks openly about money and possessions. His message conveys two sides: He strongly warns against the spiritual dangers of making money our god, and he also makes it clear that a wise use of our material possessions can enhance our relationship to God.

Jesus challenges us to dethrone money as a rival god. Martin Luther once observed, "There are three conversions necessary: the conversion of the heart, mind, and the purse." Of these three, the last conversion proves the most difficult.

Daily Practice

To express your intentions to dethrone money and to put God first in your life, bless someone today with an anonymous monetary gift.

BODY

*Do you not know that your body
is a temple of the Holy Spirit within you,
which you have from God?*
1 Corinthians 6:19

Our bodies lie at the center of our spiritual lives. This may sound strange, but it is true. We are incarnate beings in our very nature; we experience the world through our bodies.

This is why God came to earth as a human—as Jesus—and not as an angel. God came as a human being with a real body like ours. Through Jesus we see the mystery of the Incarnation: The Word became flesh and dwelt among us.

Today, through his Spirit, the Lord Jesus wants to dwell within our bodies. But he can only do this when we offer them as living sacrifices to God. This total yielding of every part of ourselves to God renews our minds and transforms our spirits.

Daily Practice

Lie on the floor facedown or faceup. Explicitly and intentionally surrender your body to God. Take time to go over each part of your body, offering everything to God.

TEMPTATION

*For we do not have a high priest who is unable to empathize
with our weaknesses, but we have one who has been tempted
in every way, just as we are—yet he did not sin.*
Hebrews 4:15, NIV

We are attacked human beings. Each day brings with it temptations and bad influences that try to undermine our relationship with God. These temptations take the form of thoughts that carry us away from the loving way of Christ.

Scripture comforts us with the knowledge that Jesus has been tempted in every way, just like we have been, yet is without sin. Jesus reminds us that temptation itself is not a sin. Nor do our temptations surprise him since he has experienced them.

Like Jesus did in the desert, we too need to face our temptations, name them, and share them with the One who alone can help us to overcome them.

Daily Practice

Take ten minutes today to create your own "desert experience"—be alone with God and bring forward those temptations with which you are presently struggling. Receive the grace that God offers as you face your temptations.

PRAY

[Jesus] was praying in a certain place, and after he had finished,
one of his disciples said to him, "Lord, teach us to
pray, as John taught his disciples."
Luke 11:1

Many people long for a firsthand, interactive relationship with God. Lacking a vital sense of the eternal in their lives, they want to know how to communicate with God. In other words, they want to learn how to pray.

The early disciples also want to know how to pray, so they ask Jesus to teach them. Significantly, this is the only time they ask to be taught anything! When they make this request, Jesus gives them what we call the Lord's Prayer. (See Luke 11:2-4.)

We can spend a lifetime learning how to pray this prayer the way Jesus teaches us. Many assume if we just say the words then we are praying. But this is far from the truth. These words need to be entered into, lived in, meditated on, as well as spoken. If we are interested in learning how to pray, Lent is a good time to begin.

Daily Practice

Meditate on the Lord's Prayer today. Slowly recite each line and consider its meaning for your life.

WILL

"Yet not as I will, but as you will."
Matthew 26:39, NIV

One of the most special gifts given to us is our will. Each of us is relatively free to make different choices, to cause things to happen that otherwise would not occur, and to act for good or for evil. This is how critical our will is.

God also has a will for our lives. The heart of our journeys as Christ-followers lies in learning how to surrender our wills to God's will. Jesus models this surrender in the verse above, and this is what Jesus invites us to do as well. In his earthly life, Jesus shows us what single-minded and wholehearted abandonment to the will of God looks like.

Surrendering our will to God does not mean that we then have no will of our own. Nor does surrender equate to resignation or passivity. Rather it means that our deepest desire is to discern, follow, and act upon what God wants for our lives. Learning how to do this is a lifelong adventure.

Daily Practice

As an expression of your desire to choose God's will for your life, sit quietly in God's presence, clench your fists tightly, and then open them slowly to the Lord.

PALM SUNDAY

Read Mark 11:1-11.

"Hosanna! Blessed is the one who comes in the name of the Lord!"
Mark 11:9

There will be moments in our lives as Jesus-followers when we need to take a stand. It might involve standing for faithfulness in our personal relationships, being honest in our business dealings, or acting with integrity in matters of morality. In the wider public arena, it could mean facing issues about inequality between the haves and the have-nots, race and gender inequality, or issues of violence and lack of justice. In these areas and countless others, we can discern what response will most express the greatest command and then act.

This is what Jesus does that first Palm Sunday. He makes his decision to enter Jerusalem. He offers witness to God's kingdom there in the Holy City. He enters the city in such a way that no one will be able to ignore him. He takes on the messianic role, the role foretold by the prophet Zechariah in the Old Testament. He arrives humbly and vulnerably, riding on a colt. This is how Jesus takes his stand, whatever the consequences. He knows that as he does this, he is not alone.

When Jesus rides into Jerusalem amid the cheering crowds, he is saying in effect, "I stand for God's kingdom. Even if I am destroyed, I will be faithful to God and to myself." Jesus can no longer condone the massive structures of evil that surround him. He knows he has to face the evil in the temple and the evil in the world, no matter what happens to him personally. If he does not, he will fail in his calling to be God's Messiah for both Israel and the world. He takes the essential first step in his final action to save all humankind.

Followers of Jesus seek to live their lives as he would. Often Lent is a good time for us to identify those things, both in ourselves and around us, that Jesus would like us to confront. Jesus decides that first Palm Sunday to take a stand for his deepest convictions. Will we do the same? We will need a combination of courage and faith. But we know that we are not on our own; God is with us.

JUDGE

"Do not judge, so that you may not be judged."
Matthew 7:1

We have the tendency to constantly judge others. Too often we judge others for faults that we struggle with ourselves. Rather than face these things in our own lives, we see them in those around us.

Jesus addresses our judgmental habits head-on in Matthew's Gospel by saying, "Why do you see the speck in your neighbor's eye, but do not notice the log in your own eye?" (7:3). Jesus explains that we must first take the log out of our own eye, and then we will be able to see the speck in the other person's eye more clearly.

Lent can be a time to confront the logs in our own eyes, to name them, and to call on the Lord for help removing them. Something beautiful happens when we do this: We become less judgmental, more gentle, and more understanding of the struggles that others face. In a word, we become *compassionate*.

Daily Practice
Write down the name of a log in your eye that you often judge in the lives of those around you. Be as honest as you can. Ask God for the grace and mercy to remove this plank and to deepen your compassion for others who wrestle with it as well.

Day 36

STRANGER

"I was a stranger and you welcomed me."
Matthew 25:35

Many people in this world feel like they are strangers. We may experience this feeling if we are in situations where we have no genuine connections with other people. This sense of disconnect can happen in our places of work, our church communities, and even our homes.

Significantly, Jesus and the New Testament writers emphasize welcoming the stranger. The writer of Hebrews maintains that when we show hospitality to strangers, we may entertain angels unaware. (See Hebrews 13:2.) Not only are we encouraged to make strangers around us feel at home, but we are also reminded that Christ comes close to us when we do.

Welcoming strangers is a basic component of discipleship. Acknowledging this make us more aware both of the strangers around us and also motivates us to reach out and welcome them.

Daily Practice
As you go through the day, look for a stranger in your midst—a new colleague at work, a visitor at church, the person who has moved in down the road. Take the initiative to say hello, reach out with an extended hand, and take an interest in this person.

BETRAY

"Truly I tell you, one of you will betray me."
Matthew 26:21

Few experiences can be more painful than betrayal. Many of us have faced betrayal in our own lives—a romantic partner has an affair, a close friend breaks confidentiality, a business partner deceives us. Such acts of betrayal cut painfully into our souls, often evoking anger and hatred.

In that unholy week leading up to his crucifixion, Jesus also experiences betrayal. Peter denies him. Judas kisses him. His other friends desert him. Because of these betrayals, Jesus' enemies capture him. From that moment on, Jesus enters his passion and faithfully fulfills his calling as the suffering servant-king.

Could our betrayals also become moments to live more passionately into our calling as followers of the Crucified One? What would it mean for us this Lent to move beyond our anger and hatred toward those who have betrayed us?

Daily Practice
Bring the pain of your betrayals to God today. How is God calling you to live with them? Make a solemn commitment that you will always seek to be faithful to the promises you have made.

Day 38 · Maundy Thursday

PRUNE

*"[The Father] removes every branch in me that bears no fruit.
Every branch that bears fruit he prunes to make it bear more fruit."*
John 15:2

Pruning helps trees bear healthy fruit. It does not make them look more beautiful, but it does make them more fruitful. Unnecessary branches must be pruned, cut off, so that the tree can produce all the fruit it can.

In his striking image of the vine and the branches, Jesus speaks of how our lives need to be pruned by God. Those parts of our lives that lead us to resist Jesus' way of love have to be stripped away. This pruning is done directly by the vinedresser, the Father, cutting the branches.

This pruning usually occurs when we experience hardship and humiliation. Through difficult times, we are challenged to recognize God's pruning hand. Only then will we be accepting of God's cleansing work in our lives instead of resisting it.

Daily Practice
Ask God to reveal to you how selfishness and self-centeredness gets expressed in your relationships. Pray for God to gently prune you of your resistance to love.

GETHSEMANE

Then Jesus went with [his disciples] to a place called Gethsemane; and he said to his disciples, "Sit here while I go over there and pray."
Matthew 26:36

We all have Gethsemane moments. Perhaps we find ourselves in a crisis of some sort or we wrestle with what God wants us to do or we face the diagnosis of a severe illness. Whatever these personal Gethsemanes may look like, they have a way of challenging our trust in God.

For Jesus, his time in the Garden of Gethsemane is a time of lonely prayer before his crucifixion. It is in Gethsemane that he surrenders his life to God. It is where he falls with his face to the ground and prays, "My Father, if it is possible, let this cup pass from me; yet not what I want but what you want" (Matt. 26:39).

May we allow our own Gethsemanes to become opportunities for us to renew our trust and confidence in God's purpose for our lives.

Daily Practice
Before you go to sleep tonight, slowly make the sign of the cross over your body as an outward sign of your heart's intention to make Jesus' prayer of surrender your own in the midst of your Gethsemane moment.

DIE

*"Very truly, I tell you, unless a grain of wheat falls
into the earth and dies, it remains just a single grain;
but if it dies, it bears much fruit."*
John 12:24

In the verse above, Jesus is primarily speaking of his own death. At first his death will appear as a tragedy, but in the end it will be a triumph. His death will be the ultimate victory of the resurrection power of God over the forces of evil, sin, and death.

Though Jesus' death is unique, he invites his followers to die as well. Like a seed that is planted in the ground and dies, Jesus invites us to die to ourselves in order to bear good fruit. We are asked to lay down our lives in love to be raised to new life.

The breathtaking message of Good Friday and Easter Sunday is that life comes out of death. The big question facing us as we journey into the events of the cross and the resurrection is this: What do we need to die to this Easter in order to enter more fully into the new life Christ wants to give us?

Daily Practice
Write down your answer to the question above on a small piece of paper, tear it up, and then bury it in the ground.

EASTER SUNDAY

Read Mark 16:1-8.

*"Do not be alarmed; you are looking for Jesus of Nazareth,
who was crucified. He has been raised; he is not here.
Look, there is the place they laid him."*
Mark 16:6

Christ is risen! He is risen indeed! This Easter greeting reminds us that God's action in raising Jesus is the bottom line of our faith. On the third day, after his crucifixion, Mary Magdalene, Mary, mother of James, and Salmone find Jesus' tomb empty. The love that Jesus proclaims, the love he lives, the love he is, is not defeated by the powers of evil and death. This is breathtakingly good news. No faith could be more tragic, no belief more futile than Christianity without its risen Lord. It would be sad and foolish to base our lives on a dead hero.

The strongest evidence for the Resurrection is the transformed lives of Jesus' disciples. How else do we explain the sudden transformation that took place in their lives? Within days those frightened and grieving disciples are transformed into bold and courageous witnesses willing to die for their faith. Something most extraordinary must have taken place for this to have happened. The One whom they follow is raised from the grave, and they encounter him in a way that convinces them he is now living beyond crucifixion.

The Resurrection means much for our lives today. Jesus is present with us as our loving Friend. He is available to each one of us in our struggle with the forces of evil. We too can experience "little Easters" in the midst of those things that make us "die" each day—the betrayal of a friend, the cruelty of a colleague, or even the failure of a dream. Easter reminds us that the risen Christ is always able to bring light and life where there seems to be only darkness and death. What wonderful good news this is! We are indeed Easter people living in a Good Friday world.

We can celebrate this good news: The risen Christ is in our midst. He continues to make available another kind of life to anyone and everyone. He has promised that all those who seek will find. May the words of Paul be our own prayer today: "I want to know Christ and the power of his resurrection and the sharing of his sufferings by becoming like him in his death" (Phil. 3:10).

CPSIA information can be obtained at www.ICGtesting.com
Printed in the USA
LVOW10s2246120216

474909LV00008B/12/P